Native Americans

Kumeyaay

Barbara A. Gray-Kanatiiosh

ABDO Publishing Company

visit us at
www.abdopublishing.com

Published by ABDO Publishing Company, 4940 Viking Drive, Edina, Minnesota 55435. Copyright © 2007 by Abdo Consulting Group, Inc. International copyrights reserved in all countries. No part of this book may be reproduced in any form without written permission from the publisher. The Checkerboard Library™ is a trademark and logo of ABDO Publishing Company.

Printed in the United States.

Cover Photo: ©2005 www.gballard.net
Interior Photos: Corbis p. 30; Getty Images p. 4; Nativestock.com pp. 29, 30
Illustrations: David Kanietakeron Fadden pp. 7, 9, 11, 13, 15, 17, 19, 21, 23, 25, 27
Editors: Rochelle Baltzer, Heidi M. Dahmes
Art Direction & Maps: Neil Klinepier

Library of Congress Cataloging-in-Publication Data

Gray-Kanatiiosh, Barbara A., 1963-
  Kumeyaay / Barbara A. Gray-Kanatiiosh.
    p. cm. -- (Native Americans)
  Includes index.
  ISBN-13: 978-1-59197-655-4
  ISBN-10: 1-59197-655-3
  1. Kamia Indians--History--Juvenile literature. 2. Kamia Indians--Social life and customs--Juvenile literature. I. Title.

E99.K18G73 2007
973.04'97572--dc22

                                                                    2006021132

About the Author: Barbara A. Gray-Kanatiiosh, JD
Barbara Gray-Kanatiiosh, JD, Ph.D. ABD, is an Akwesasne Mohawk. She resides at the Mohawk Nation and is of the Wolf Clan. She has a Juris Doctorate from Arizona State University, where she was one of the first recipients of ASU's special certificate in Indian Law. Barbara's Ph.D. is in Justice Studies at ASU. She is currently working on her dissertation, which concerns the impacts of environmental injustice on indigenous culture. Barbara works hard to educate children about Native Americans through her writing and Web site, where children may ask questions and receive a written response about the Haudenosaunee culture. The Web site is: www.peace4turtleisland.org

About the Illustrator: David Kanietakeron Fadden
David Kanietakeron Fadden is a member of the Akwesasne Mohawk Wolf Clan. His work has appeared in publications such as *Akwesasne Notes*, *Indian Time*, and the *Northeast Indian Quarterly*. Examples of his work have also appeared in various publications of the Six Nations Indian Museum in Onchiota, NY. His work has also appeared in "How the West Was Lost: Always the Enemy," produced by Gannett Production, which appeared on the Discovery Channel. David's work has been exhibited in Albany, NY; the Lake Placid Center for the Arts; Centre Strathearn in Montreal, Quebec; North Country Community College in Saranac Lake, NY; Paul Smith's College in Paul Smiths, NY; and at the Unison Arts & Learning Center in New Paltz, NY.

Contents

Where They Lived

The Kumeyaay (KOO-mee-eye) homelands were located in southern California. Tribal territory included present-day Imperial and San Diego **counties**. The area also stretched into Mexico. Neighboring tribes included the Cahuilla, Gabrielino, Luiseño, and Cupeño. The Kumeyaay spoke a **dialect** from the Hokan branch of the Yuman language.

Many different landforms covered Kumeyaay territory. Beaches and salt marshes lined the Pacific coast. Inland, there were mountains, canyons, and valleys. Marshes and lakes were also found inland, as were seasonal streams and creeks.

Various plants and animals lived in the forests, grasslands, and deserts of Kumeyaay land. Shrubs, berries, and wildflowers were abundant there. And, oak trees were plentiful. These trees provided acorns, which were a dependable food source for the tribe.

Oak trees were found in grassy valleys on Kumeyaay land.

At certain times of the year, Kumeyaay lands experienced dry weather. At these times, food and water weren't readily available. So when it rained, the Kumeyaay found ways to make use of the rainwater. They built special paths to direct the water to their villages. This ensured that they had sufficient water.

Kumeyaay Homelands

Society

Kumeyaay society was divided into bands, which owned certain territories within tribal land. Between 5 and 15 family groups belonged to a band.

Each band had its own *kwaaypaay*, or leader. This title usually belonged to a family and was passed on from father to son. But sometimes, the title went to a man outside the family if he had superior leadership skills.

The kwaaypaay had many responsibilities. He assigned duties and handled disagreements among the band. A helper called a *koreau* assisted him. The koreau organized meetings, trips, and daily activities.

A council of talented men and women helped the kwaaypaay make decisions. Council members were often priests, scientists, or doctors. These people healed others and performed ceremonies.

The council also passed down history and **cultural** teachings through bird songs. These sacred songs taught other tribal members traditions and morals. To prepare for singing and leading these songs, council members participated in special ceremonies. It took lifelong devotion to learn bird songs.

The Kumeyaay used trade routes for communication between villages and bands. People called runners quickly relayed information over far distances.

Food

The Kumeyaay obtained food in several ways. They hunted, fished, gardened, and gathered. To determine where and when to do these tasks, they studied the stars. The position of the stars in the sky let the Kumeyaay know the right time to take certain foods.

Men used bows and arrows to hunt deer, antelope, and bighorn sheep. They also tracked small animals. Using traps or snares, the men captured badgers, rabbit, rodents, and birds. Kumeyaay families fished in the bays. There, they also gathered shellfish and seaweed.

Inland, the Kumeyaay grew foods such as corn, beans, and squashes. The men burned down trees to prepare fields for planting. Then, the tribe planted foods in areas where rainfall was abundant.

Usually, the women gathered foods. In spring and summer, they collected plants, fruits, seed, and berries. They gathered acorns and piñon nuts in autumn.

The Kumeyaay used several methods to prepare food for eating. The women ground seed and nuts to make flour and bread. They cooked some foods over fire. Acorn mush and soups were heated in baskets over hot rocks.

Other foods were dried in the sun or stored in pots or baskets for later use. The Kumeyaay kept acorns in large woven baskets called granaries. Granaries protected food from being eaten by insects and animals.

Before eating acorns, a poisonous mix of chemicals called tannic acid had to be removed. To do this, the Kumeyaay poured water over acorn meal until the acid washed out.

9

Homes

The Kumeyaay had both summer and winter villages. This was because they **migrated** at certain times of the year. Access to food and water was very important when choosing a village location. For this reason, the tribe settled near rivers and streams.

Kumeyaay homes were dome-shaped. They were built over a dug-out area lined with boulders. The Kumeyaay constructed the frame of the dome with willow poles. They bent the poles and used twine to tie them together at the top. Then, they attached **thatch** to the frame.

A Kumeyaay home had a small opening for a doorway covered with **tule** mats. Inside, soft grass covered the floor. The Kumeyaay kept a small fire burning to heat the home. When it was still cold, they slept under rabbit-fur blankets.

The center of a Kumeyaay village had a circular space where religious gatherings took place. Village leaders lived in this area and managed the gatherings.

Kumeyaay villages also contained sweat houses. These buildings were constructed like homes, but they were smaller. Inside, there was a fire pit where the men heated rocks. Then, they poured water over the rocks to make steam. Kumeyaay men used sweat houses both to meet and to purify themselves.

Kumeyaay villages were built around a circular space that was used for sacred gatherings. Brush-covered structures provided shade during these ceremonies.

Clothing

Kumeyaay clothing was made from plants and animals. Women wore skirts woven from willow bark. Men wore waist cords made from plant fibers. These belts resembled netting. The men used them to hold tools. During winter, both men and women wore robes for extra warmth. The robes were made from animal hides or furs.

The Kumeyaay wore basket hats for protection and decoration. Underneath them, they kept their hair long. The men wore their hair loose or tied up in a knot. Women had bangs. After a family member's death, relatives cut their hair short as a symbol of mourning.

To decorate their bodies, the Kumeyaay **tattooed** and painted themselves. Women tattooed their chins and sometimes their arms or chests. Men occasionally tattooed their legs. Both men and women painted their faces and bodies for ceremonies.

Kumeyaay clothing was practical. Men's belts provided a place to hold tools. And, basket hats were used to carry items.

13

Crafts

Kumeyaay women made baskets and pottery. They used bone **awls** to weave baskets from plants, such as willow, sumac, and grass. Basket patterns often included butterflies, flowers, deer, and rattlesnakes.

The baskets served several purposes. Some were used for gifting and trading. Others were used for cooking and storing foods. Kumeyaay women used seed-beater baskets to gather seed. These baskets were small, tightly woven, and attached to a long stick. When women pushed them into seed-bearing plants, seed fell into them.

Kumeyaay women also constructed cradleboards to carry babies. Cradleboards were woven from willow and padded with leaves and grass. Women hung them from trees while working. And, they rested the cradleboards on their backs while traveling.

The Kumeyaay also made clay pottery. They found clay along riverbanks. Then, they formed pots by coiling the clay. Next, they smoothed the sides of the pots. Finally, they fired the pots to harden the clay. The finished pots were used for holding water, as well as for cooking or storing foods.

It was believed that a pot would crack if anyone saw it being made. So, pottery making was usually a solitary activity.

15

Family

When a Kumeyaay woman married, she left her home to live with her husband. She kept her family name. However, the couple's children took their father's family name.

To keep their bands strong, men and women were in charge of specific tasks. The women gathered and prepared foods. They also made crafts and clothing. Kumeyaay men built tools, hunted, and prepared fields for gardening.

When the Kumeyaay came together for ceremonies, they often played games. Most games provided practice for the skills needed in their community. Common games involved throwing sticks through hoops and targets. The Kumeyaay also ran races to prove their strength and endurance.

But some games were simply for fun. The tribe especially enjoyed *peon*, which is still played today. In this game, members of one team hide bones or sticks behind them. Then, the opposing team guesses which hands are hiding the objects. *Peon* ends when one team has all of the bones or sticks. The game can last for days.

The Kumeyaay studied the
stars to determine when
to have ceremonies.

Children

All family members helped raise and teach Kumeyaay children. Adults taught the children tribal stories, songs, and dances. Boys and girls learned daily tasks by helping their **extended family**.

Kumeyaay children needed to understand nature. Boys and girls learned how to read the stars to know when to gather foods. Adults taught children where to collect foods and how to preserve them.

Women taught the girls how to weave clothing, baskets, and blankets. Kumeyaay girls also learned how to sculpt pots. The women showed them where to gather the necessary materials for these activities.

Men taught the boys how to make fishing equipment, such as nets, hooks, spears, and lines. Boys also learned to make boats. To do this, they tied **tule** together. Then, adults used asphaltum to waterproof the boats. The men also showed the boys how to catch fish and dig for shellfish.

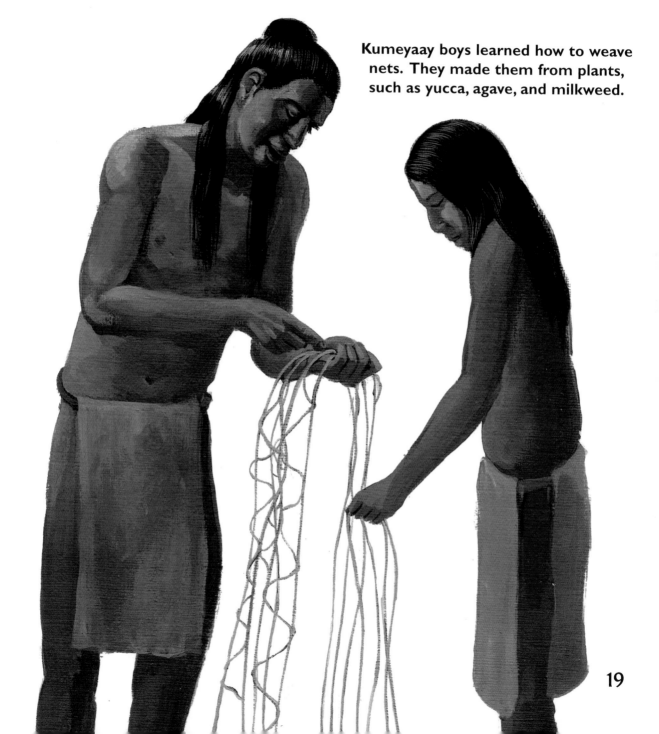

Kumeyaay boys learned how to weave nets. They made them from plants, such as yucca, agave, and milkweed.

19

Myths

There are many myths in the Kumeyaay **culture**. The following is part of a Kumeyaay creation story. It explains how life came into being on Earth.

Long ago, salt water covered Earth. Two brothers lived beneath the water. One day, the older brother came to the surface. He saw nothing but salt water. So, he wanted to create beings.

First, he made little red ants. The ants filled the water until their bodies merged together and became land. Then, he created black birds with flat bills. But, he noticed the birds could not see because it was too dark.

He needed to create light. So, he formed a circle of red, yellow, and black clay. He threw it into the sky, and it became the moon. Next, he threw another clay circle into the sky to create the sun.

Then, the older brother wanted to create human beings. So, he formed a man from a light-colored piece of clay. He made a woman from the rib of the man. The children of this man and woman were called *ipai*, or people. They lived in a great mountain called *Wikami*.

According to
Kumeyaay myth,
a man who lived
in the sea
created living
beings from clay.

War

The Kumeyaay were friendly people. Their lifestyle depended on keeping peaceful relations with nearby tribes. They often traded items with their neighbors.

However when peace efforts failed, the Kumeyaay were prepared to fight. Sometimes, war was necessary to protect their land and people. If Kumeyaay territory was invaded, war would likely break out.

The Kumeyaay often **ambushed** their enemies. When fighting, they used war clubs and bows and arrows. Their war clubs were cylinder shaped. Their bows were made of willow and had strings made from **sinew**. Arrowheads were made from stone or wood. These were attached to the arrows with asphaltum.

Prior to European contact, war did not always lead to death. Sometimes, the Kumeyaay were satisfied simply to chase away an enemy.

Yet after European contact, some of the traditional Kumeyaay war methods changed. The tribe began using horses and guns during battle. This made war more deadly.

Prior to European contact, Kumeyaay warriors used weapons made from wood and obsidian. Obsidian is a hard, glassy rock that forms when lava cools.

23

Contact with Europeans

In 1542, Portuguese explorer Juan Rodríguez Cabrillo led an expedition along the California coast. The Kumeyaay were the first Native Americans to see his ships sail into the San Diego Bay.

More than two hundred years later, Spanish **missionaries** entered Kumeyaay territory. They wanted to build missions and convert Native Americans to Christianity.

Unfortunately, Spanish influence put Kumeyaay ways of life at risk. The Spaniards took land from the tribe. Their agricultural habits harmed traditional Kumeyaay foods. And, they banned tribal spiritual practices. Some Kumeyaay fled to the mountains to escape.

In 1769, Father Junípero Serra founded the San Diego Mission. Around this time, tensions were running high between the Kumeyaay and the Spanish. As a result, the Kumeyaay destroyed the San Diego Mission. However, the mission was soon rebuilt at another location.

The Kumeyaay were also harmed by foreign diseases that the Spanish settlers brought with them. At that time, Native Americans had no defenses against these illnesses. So, smallpox and the measles spread through Kumeyaay land and took thousands of lives.

Spanish missionaries captured many Kumeyaay and made them work very hard for minimal earnings.

Jane Dumas

Jane Dumas is a valued elder and a modern Kumeyaay leader from the Jamul Indian Village. She is one of the few remaining keepers of traditional tribal knowledge. So, she is often called upon to answer questions about Kumeyaay traditions.

Dumas holds a deep understanding of Kumeyaay medicinal uses of plants. Her mother was a medicine woman and taught Dumas how to find medicine plants. She also taught Dumas each plant's healing powers and preparation methods.

In addition to her expertise in traditional medicine, Dumas also knows ceremonial traditions and preparations. She helps to ensure that ceremonies are properly performed throughout the Kumeyaay community.

Dumas helped to found the San Diego American Indian Health Center in 1981. The center provides various medical services for Native Americans. Dumas worked there for more than 20 years.

In 2002, Dumas was welcomed into the first San Diego **County** Women's Hall of Fame. She was chosen for her lasting contributions to the Native American community. She gained recognition once more when she was honored as the 2005 American Indian of the Year. Dumas continues to share her knowledge in classrooms and at public events. She is a bridge maker between Native Americans and non-Native Americans.

Dumas enjoys helping to preserve Kumeyaay ways of life. She is one of the last remaining Kumeyaay that can speak the tribe's language clearly and easily.

The Kumeyaay Today

Today, many Kumeyaay live on traditional lands. There are 17 **federally recognized** Kumeyaay **reservations**. The reservations are located in present-day California and Mexico. Some of these reservations include Barona, Campo, Jamul, La Huerta, Mesa Grande, San Pasqual, and Viejas.

The Kumeyaay work hard to preserve their **culture**. They continue to make pottery and baskets. Basket-making methods are passed down from tribal elders. Today, Kumeyaay coiled baskets are considered some of the finest in the world.

Bird songs still serve an important purpose in Kumeyaay culture. These songs are performed at funerals, memorials, and certain ceremonies. When performing, the singers do not use drums. Instead, they use traditional rattles filled with native palm seed. Sadly, many songs have been lost throughout the years. This makes the remaining bird songs sacred.

To preserve and pass on tribal knowledge, the Kumeyaay have created a non-profit organization. Kumeyaay.com provides the public with correct information about tribal history and culture. The Web site also serves to unite the bands within the Kumeyaay tribe.

A group of Kumeyaay men sang traditional songs and used gourd rattles during a cultural presentation at the San Diego Museum of Man in May 2003.

Anthony Pico, chairman of the Viejas Band of Kumeyaay Indians, believes that tribal leaders should educate the public about modern Native Americans. Pico works to correctly represent his people.

Animal patterns, such as the deer on this coiled storage basket, still appear on modern Kumeyaay basketry.

Kumeyaay pottery was rarely decorated. If a pot had a design, it was usually of dots, lines, stars, or geometric shapes.

Glossary

ambush - a surprise attack from a hidden position.

awl - a pointed tool for making small holes in materials such as leather or wood.

county - the largest local government within a state of the United States.

culture - the customs, arts, and tools of a nation or people at a certain time.

dialect - a form of a language spoken in a certain area or by certain people.

extended family - a family that includes grandparents, uncles, aunts, and cousins in addition to a mother, father, and children.

federal recognition - the U.S. government's recognition of a tribe as being an independent nation. The tribe is then eligible for special funding and for protection of its reservation lands.

migrate - to move from one place to another, often to find food.

mission - a center or headquarters for religious work. A missionary is a person who spreads a church's religion.

reservation - a piece of land set aside by the government for Native Americans to live on.

sinew - a band of tough fibers that joins a muscle to a bone.

tattoo - a permanent design made on the skin.

thatch - woven mats made of grass.

tule - a type of reed that grows in wetlands. Tule is native to California.

Web Sites

To learn more about the Kumeyaay, visit ABDO Publishing Company on the World Wide Web at **www.abdopublishing.com**. Web sites about the Kumeyaay are featured on our Book Links page. These links are routinely monitored and updated to provide the most current information available.

Index